CHRISTO AND JEANNE-CLAUDE
WRAP THE WORLD

The Story of Two Groundbreaking Environmental Artists

G. Neri

illustrated by
Elizabeth Haidle

CANDLEWICK PRESS

THE ARTIST CHRISTO
was a poor refugee from Eastern Europe whose father once ran a fabric factory.

JEANNE-CLAUDE was the rich stepdaughter of a French general, who was only interested in the cadets who asked her to dance.

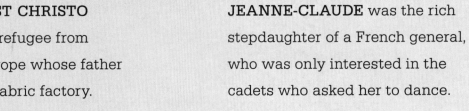

They met at her home in Paris.

"Look, Papa. Mama brought home a stray dog," teased Jeanne-Claude.

"Hush," said the general. "He's here to paint our portraits."

As Christo was packing up to leave, Jeanne-Claude wandered over to talk to the artist. "I know nothing about art," she told him.

"Have you ever been to the Louvre?" he asked. "It's the finest museum in Paris."

"Oh, they have art there?" She laughed. "We used to sneak in to roller-skate from room to room there when I was a kid."

Christo smiled. *She's funny and rebellious*, he thought. A rule-breaker, just like him.

He persuaded her to come to the Louvre so he could teach her about all its classic paintings, drawings, and sculptures. But she was bored by the stuffy old museum.

Christo had to admit he was, too. "You know, I paint portraits in the old style to pay the rent," he told her. "But my real art is quite daring. As soon as I can, I'll stop painting portraits and only do work that is bold."

"What about paying the rent?" she asked.

"Art is much bigger than money," he answered. "Money is not life. Freedom is. And art is freedom."

After climbing seven flights of stairs, Jeanne-Claude was surprised when Christo opened the door to his tiny room. "Why are you wrapping these silly objects in cloth and rope?" asked Jeanne-Claude.

"Why not?" said Christo. "It's art."

"That's not art."

"Says who?" asked Christo. "Art is supposed to make you see things differently."

"How does wrapping a bottle or a can do that?" asked Jeanne-Claude. "Besides . . . it's ugly."

"Look: you drink from a bottle every day, yes? So what?" asked Christo. "But now I wrap it—and voilà!

"Suddenly you think: What is this? What's really under there? What color is it? What does it hold?

"The object has kept its shape, but now you are unsure. It has become a mystery."

"Oh, I get it. It's revealing—while concealing."

"YES!" shouted Christo.

Jeanne-Claude gazed at his wrapped objects. "Here's a question: If you can wrap cans and bottles, why not wrap everything?"

That's when they fell in love.

Once they were married and had a son, Cyril, they had
no money for materials, so anything that wasn't nailed
down became art.

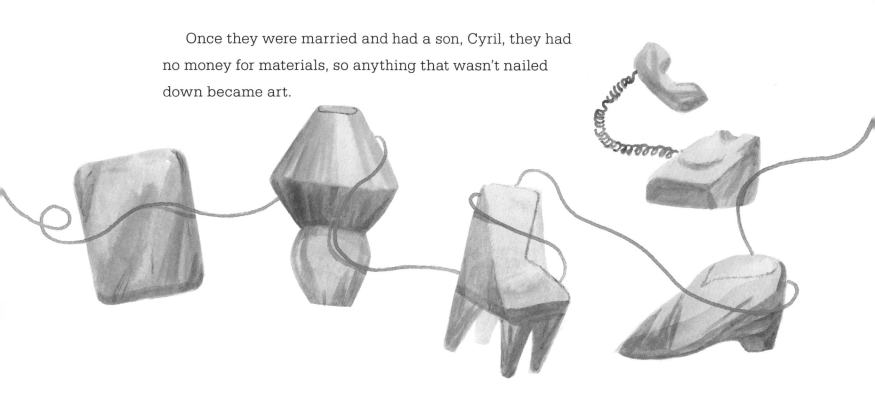

It was irrational and bold—it defied explanation!
What does it mean? Why is it covered?
Packages are meant to be opened—but not these!

For their first official outdoor collaboration, Christo and Jeanne-Claude were inspired by seeing giant rolls of industrial paper on a dock. They asked the dockworkers to arrange them and then wrapped them in a tarp.

DOCKSIDE PACKAGES, 1961

Was it art? Some people thought so; others not.

People loved it or hated it. They got it or didn't. For Christo and Jeanne-Claude, the arguments only added to the art. The point was, people weren't walking through life blindly. They were looking and questioning *everything*.

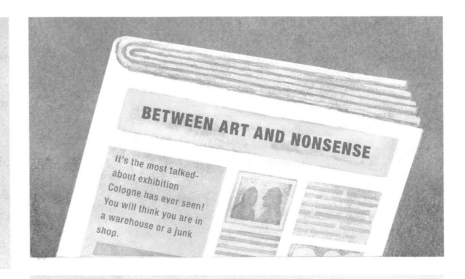

BETWEEN ART AND NONSENSE

It's the most talked-about exhibition Cologne has ever seen! You will think you are in a warehouse or a junk shop.

Is this art?

Art is anything that's made by an artist, so yes.

Once, when they needed an extra piece for a show, they experimented by wrapping a real live woman! The breathable plastic wrap obscured her features, making her appear no longer human but a sculpture.

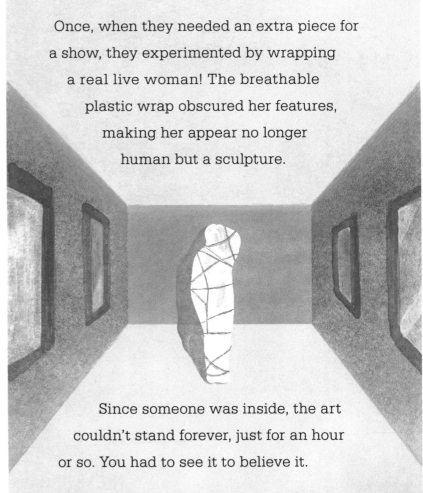

Since someone was inside, the art couldn't stand forever, just for an hour or so. You had to see it to believe it.

Word spread. The memory was bigger than the sculpture itself!
That got Christo and Jeanne-Claude thinking.

What if *all* our art was temporary, my love? Why should it be trapped in a dusty museum forever?

Yes, it should be more of an experience. It should live in your memory like a dream.

Or a fable, like "Once upon a time . . ."

So they decided to make a public event that was truly unforgettable—something that would literally stop traffic and force people to experience it. They built a fourteen-foot-tall wall out of barrels and blocked the street!

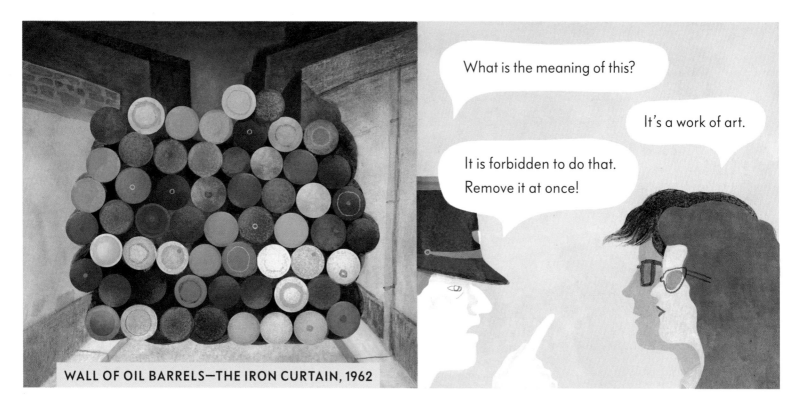

WALL OF OIL BARRELS—THE IRON CURTAIN, 1962

What is the meaning of this?

It's a work of art.

It is forbidden to do that. Remove it at once!

Jeanne-Claude made a deal with the police: They would keep it up till midnight, *then* take it down. It would be like it never happened.

Some people saw it as an annoyance. Others as a protest against the creation of the Berlin Wall, which tore the city in two. But one thing was for sure: what was once a boring old street became the talk of the town.

After this success, Christo and Jeanne-Claude started to dream big.
And to dream big, there was only one place to go: America.

New York was full of fancy storefronts, but Jeanne-Claude and Christo were too poor to do more than window-shop. So they built their own storefronts out of junk they found on the street and draped the windows so no one could see in. People started buying them.

We should wrap something big. Something monumental!

Christo and Jeanne-Claude didn't always agree. Sometimes they fought over ideas; other times, they had the same idea at once. But their arguments always made their art stronger.

WRAPPED MUSEUM OF CONTEMPORARY ART, CHICAGO, 1969

"People look at their surroundings all the time, but they don't really *see* them," said Christo. "When we wrap architecture, it becomes sculpture. *Then* they see it."

Why not a wall?

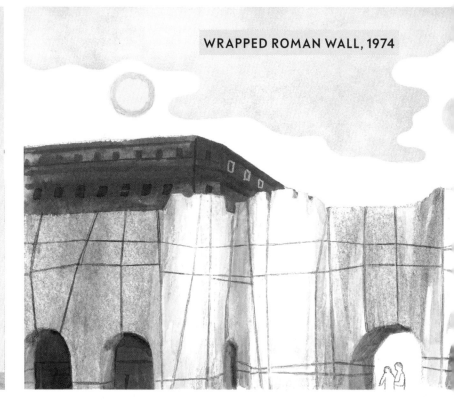

WRAPPED ROMAN WALL, 1974

THE PONT NEUF WRAPPED, 1985

How about . . .

a bridge?

Or the German Parliament building!

It was all monumental. And when people had only two weeks to experience it, it became even more special. Was it ever really there, or was it all a dream? It became a myth, a tall tale.

"Do you remember when—?" people would say.

"Oh, I was there! I saw that!"

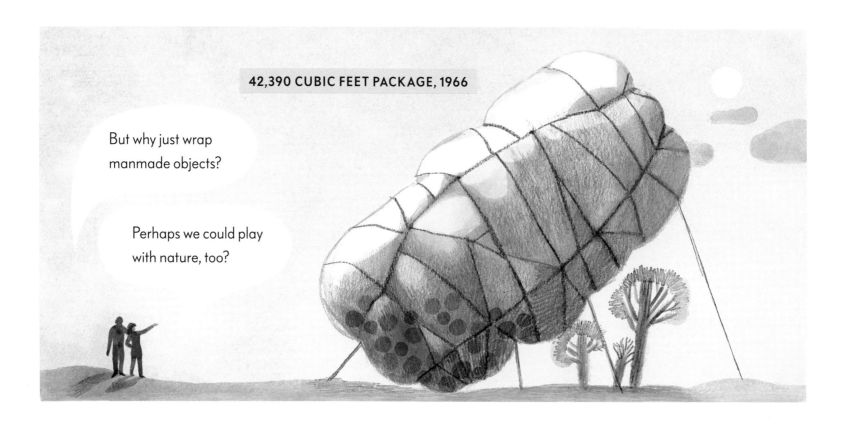

42,390 CUBIC FEET PACKAGE, 1966

But why just wrap manmade objects?

Perhaps we could play with nature, too?

Could they package air?   Wrap a coast?   Cover the ocean?   Bundle a grove of trees?

WRAPPED COAST, 1969

OCEAN FRONT, 1974

Why not? The crowds came to see what all the fuss was about. The projects made people smile or made them mad. They made people see again.

WRAPPED TREES, 1998

Each project grew bigger and bigger; the more ambitious and expensive a project was, the more absurd the process became. Projects took years to realize, cost millions of dollars, and involved thousands of people fighting for, and *against*, them.

Christo was delighted. "The people's reactions are part of the art, too!"

They sold Christo's sketches of their projects to pay for everything so they didn't have to rely on ticket sales, sponsorships, or government funding—they could create whatever they wanted. For Christo and Jeanne-Claude, their art was like a scream of freedom.

They wondered, "What if you loosened the fabric—let it flow and breathe like nature?" Could they . . .

hang a giant curtain across a valley?

VALLEY CURTAIN, 1972

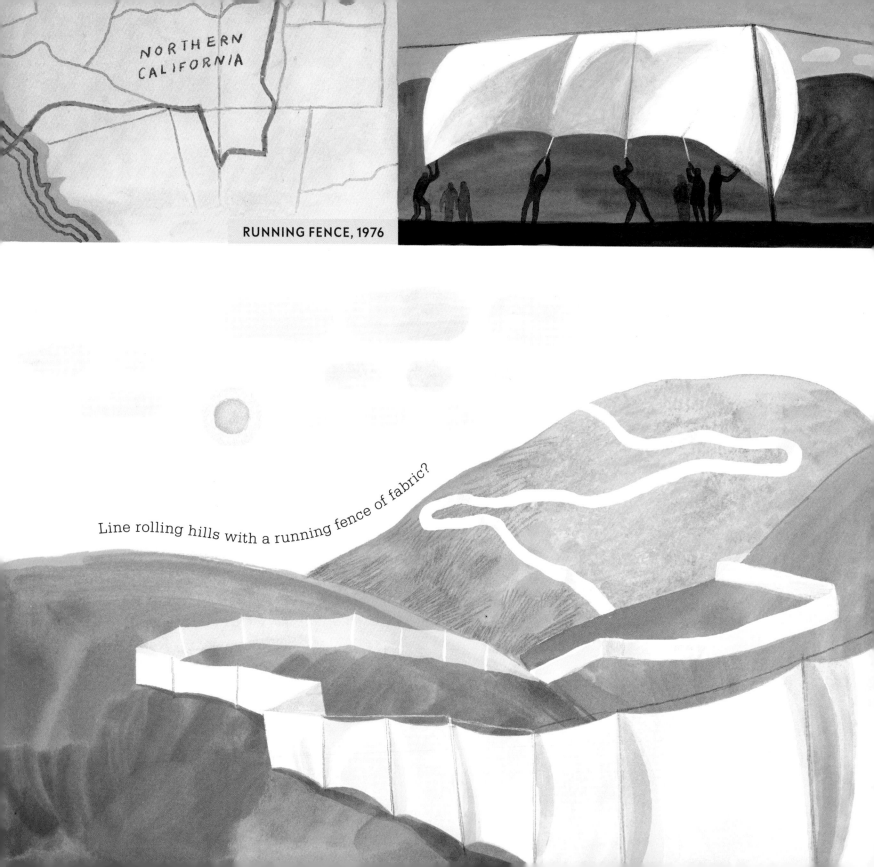

NORTHERN CALIFORNIA

RUNNING FENCE, 1976

Line rolling hills with a running fence of fabric?

Surround some islands in pink?

BISCAYNE BAY

SURROUNDED ISLANDS, 1983

THE UMBRELLAS, 1991

Scatter colorful umbrellas like flowers?

Build a floating path on a lake?

LAKE ISEO

THE FLOATING PIERS, 2016

As they grew older and their love grew deeper, the fabrics loosened and became more colorful. The ropes became less binding. Their art went from dark to light.

They gave up trying to control nature and gave in to nature's unpredictable energy to make the artwork even more surprising and beautiful.

People changed when they saw their projects. Their faces filled with wonder. They started to smile and talk to complete strangers about this once-in-a-lifetime event. They became like children, seeing with fresh eyes.

But why does it have to disappear after only two weeks?

Why not? Do you question a rainbow coming and going? Do you say, "Oh, I'll look at it tomorrow"?

"No, the time is now," said Jeanne-Claude. "You
have to see it to believe it. Isn't that right, my love?"

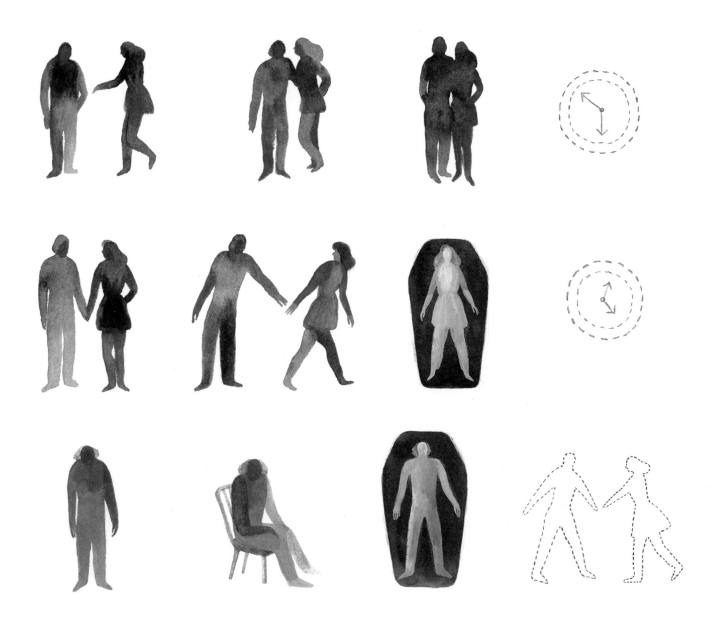

"That's right, my darling. Nothing lasts forever."

L'ARC DE TRIOMPHE, WRAPPED, 2021

ABOUT CHRISTO AND JEANNE-CLAUDE

Christo and Jeanne-Claude were born at the same hour on the same day of the same year: June 13, 1935. He was born in Bulgaria, she in Morocco. They met in Paris when Jeanne-Claude's mother commissioned Christo to paint her family's portraits. Jeanne-Claude was the stepdaughter of a general who had served with the Free French army during World War II; her mother had fought for the French Resistance against the Germans. Christo was an artist without a country after he escaped Communist Bulgaria on a railcar. He was lonely and poor, but he had grand visions for his art. When Christo and Jeanne-Claude were twenty-three, they fell in love. They had a son, Cyril, and made art together throughout their lives.

In addition to using fabric and rope to alter reality, Christo and Jeanne-Claude made art out of oil barrels, wool, and fake storefronts. They became environmental artists, as many of their outdoor works were in dialogue with nature: water, wind, and sun affected a project's look and feel; it was always changing. Their biggest goal was to make art for everyday people who don't go to museums. Instead, their art came to the people. And the people helped shape it by their involvement, whether it was in support or protest. The discussion was part of the artwork itself.

Christo and Jeanne-Claude's public art projects have been experienced by millions of people all over the world, from the shores of Australia to islands off the Florida coast to the great cities of Europe and the rolling hills of Japan. Some projects took decades to get off the ground. They cost millions of dollars and required the talents of hundreds of people, from engineers and lawyers to government and environmental officials to planners and construction work-ers. At the time of this writing, their last project to be built was *L'Arc de Triomphe, Wrapped*, which took fifty-nine years to complete. When asked how they could wait so long, Jeanne-Claude said, "It's not a matter of patience, it's a matter of passion."

Christo and Jeanne-Claude paid for every element of every project themselves by selling prints and original sketches of their proposed pieces, never asking for a cent of public money. In return, they made their art free for everyone to experience.

Jeanne-Claude passed away in 2009. Christo continued to make their projects a reality until he passed away, in 2020. It is hoped that the one remaining project, *The Mastaba*, will be realized sometime in the future in the desert of Liwa, south of Abu Dhabi.

〰〰〰

AUTHOR'S NOTE

This book is designed to be a dialogue that showcases how Christo and Jeanne-Claude's art evolved over the course of their life together. Some of the dialogue is quoting things they actually said (or close to it), but sometimes, as a narrative device, I've put their ideas into the context of a conversation to illustrate their back-and-forth in critical discussions and highlight the concepts they played with. If you would like to see specific citations for individual quotes, source notes can be found online at www.gregneri.com/home/#/christo.

All my profound thanks to Christo and Jeanne-Claude, whom I met briefly in the 2000s, shortly after their triumph with *The Gates*. Hearing them talk about freedom through art hit me deeply, and their expression of it, both in conversation and in practice, was living proof of the power of ideas. I was extremely fortunate to be perhaps the last person to interview Christo before he died, in May 2020. I will be forever grateful for having that moment before he passed on to the next world (and that he connected with my short animated film about Picasso: wow). Many thanks to Jeanne-Claude's nephew and office manager, Jonathan Henery, for taking the time to review this manuscript for accuracy and to Lorenza Giovanelli, Christo's studio manager, for being my advocate in research.

〰〰〰

THESE PROJECTS are absolutely irrational. Nobody needs a *Valley Curtain*
or a *Running Fence*. They do not exist because the president of a republic
would like to have them.... They exist because *we* want them.
They have total freedom. —*Christo*

THE FIRST reaction we get to our art is: "You want to do *what*?"
—*Jeanne-Claude*

FUN FACTS ABOUT CHRISTO AND JEANNE-CLAUDE

~~~~~~

- Christo and Jeanne-Claude lived at the same address in Manhattan from 1964, when they immigrated to New York, to the time of their deaths. Christo's studio was on the fifth floor of their narrow building, which had no elevator.

- Christo worked alone in his studio, always standing up, and he even did his own framing. Because Christo and Jeanne-Claude worked with so many people at the sites of projects, Christo's studio was the only place where he could be alone to work in peace.

- Christo and Jeanne-Claude never flew in the same airplane because if it crashed, the surviving spouse could carry on their work.

- Up until 1994, all the couple's projects were attributed to Christo only because it was easier to sell art by one name. After their projects became world-famous, they retroactively revealed that all their outdoor projects from 1961 on were created by both Christo and Jeanne-Claude.

- They refused to commercialize their work. They once turned down a million-dollar payment for a sixty-second commercial on Japanese television.

- Reporters asked them why they would spend all their money on art that wasn't for sale and only lasted two weeks. Jeanne-Claude expressed frustration with the question: "If [Christo] were to buy me a four-million-dollar diamond, this would be perfectly all right. But I don't happen to like diamonds. I prefer to have *The Gates* project, or a *Running Fence*, or a *Valley Curtain*."

- They worked an average of thirteen hours a day, seven days a week. They did not take vacations.

- Christo and Jeanne-Claude had one son, Cyril, who works with his wife, Mary Wilkinson, as a writer, photographer, filmmaker, and animal rights activist and travels the world creating art, much as his parents did. He took his father's name as his last name. On whether he ever felt neglected: "The projects are my brothers and sisters. What can I say?"

- Christo grew up around fabric. His father worked in a textile factory in Bulgaria, devising a special chemical solution used to prepare new fabric, and later opened his own factory.

- Wrapping was a big deal for Christo. His family in Bulgaria didn't wrap presents, as it wasn't a tradition there, so he was envious of this idea.

- Once, a gallery showed a piece of theirs, a wheelbarrow carrying a wrapped package, in its front window. It caused a big controversy. The town's mayor said, "It was junk. Putting it in a window and calling it art was preposterous and offensive." Later the Museum of Modern Art in New York City, one of the most prestigious art museums in the world, bought it.

- Christo and Jeanne-Claude had a sense of humor about their art. They started sending out wrapped boxes in the mail to collectors. If the collector opened the box, the art was gone! Inside was a photo of the wrapped box and a note: "You asked me to send you a package. I have sent it to you, but you have destroyed it. Keep the photograph as a souvenir."

- Once, a child saw Christo on television wrapping a car. Later he brought a toy car to Christo as a gift. Christo was so touched that the boy would sacrifice his toy that he not only wrapped it, but he also glued it to a wood backing and signed it. He found out later the toy car had belonged to the boy's brother, who was not too pleased!

- Because of their projects' often grand scale and proximity to cities, many took decades to realize. Some never received permission to proceed. In the couple's last fifty years, they realized twenty-three projects and failed to realize forty-seven. The longest a project ever took was fifty-nine years: *L'Arc de Triomphe, Wrapped* started in 1962, when Christo lived right near the monument and sketched what it would look like wrapped. It was realized in 2021.

- Sizes of crowds: 1.5 million people visited *The Floating Piers*, 3 million visited *The Umbrellas*, 4 million visited *The Gates*, 5 million visited *Wrapped Reichstag*, and 6 million showed up to see *L'Arc de Triomphe, Wrapped*, their latest project.

- *Running Fence* is considered to be the largest artwork ever created: 24.5 miles (39.4 kilometers) long, using 2.15 million square feet (200,000 square meters) of fabric.

- All materials used in temporary public art pieces were recycled and never sold or autographed. The project that used the most material was *Surrounded Islands*. And before the work was installed, approximately 40 tons of garbage were removed from the site.

BIBLIOGRAPHY

~~~~~~~

BOOKS

Baal-Teshuva, Jacob. *Christo and Jeanne-Claude*. Cologne, Germany: Taschen, 2016.

Chernow, Burt. *Christo and Jeanne-Claude: An Authorized Biography*. New York: St. Martin's Griffin, 2005.

ING Art Center. *Christo and Jeanne-Claude: Urban Projects*. Dortmund, Germany: Kettler, 2017.

Koddenberg, Matthis. *Christo and Jeanne-Claude: Early Works 1958–64*. Bönen, Germany: Kettler, 2009.

———. *Christo and Jeanne-Claude: In/Out Studio*. Bönen, Germany: Kettler, 2014.

FILMS

Blackwood, Michael. *Christo and Jeanne-Claude*. DVD. New York: Michael Blackwood Productions, 1995.

———. *Christo: Works in Progress*. DVD. New York: Michael Blackwood Productions, 1978.

DW.com. *The Art of Wrapping*. Video. 2016. https://www.dw.com/en/the-art-of-wrapping/a-36641068.

Ferrera, Antonio. *Nomad of Art: A Film Montage*. Video. 2010. https://vimeo.com/34776018.

Maysles, Albert and David. *5 Films About Christo and Jeanne-Claude*. Includes *Christo's Valley Curtain*, *Running Fence*, *Islands*, *Christo in Paris*, and *Umbrellas*. DVD set. New York: Plexifilm, 2004.

Maysles, Albert and David, Antonio Ferrera, and Matthew Prinzing. *The Gates*. Film. New York: Maysles Films, 2007.

WEBSITE

Christo and Jeanne-Claude website. https://christojeanneclaude.net/.

For Maggie—my partner in art,
who also shares a birthday
with Christo and Jeanne-Claude
GN

〰〰〰〰〰

Text copyright © 2023 by G. Neri

Illustrations copyright © 2023 by Elizabeth Haidle

First edition 2023

Library of Congress Catalog Card Number 2022936764

ISBN 978-1-5362-1661-5

23 24 25 26 27 28 CCP 10 9 8 7 6 5 4 3 2 1

Printed in Shenzhen, Guangdong, China

This book was typeset in URW Egyptienne and Bauer Grotesk.

The illustrations were done in mixed media and finished digitally.

Candlewick Press

99 Dover Street

Somerville, Massachusetts 02144

www.candlewick.com